Pocket Guide to the Old Testament

Harold Shaw Publishers
Wheaton, Illinois

Compiled from *The Shaw Pocket Bible Handbook*, edited by Walter A. Elwell. Copyright © 1984 by Harold Shaw Publishers.

ISBN 0-87788-654-7

Cover photo © Robert Cushman Hayes

First printing: February 1990

INTRODUCTION

The Old Testament consists of 39 books that were written over a period of about a thousand years. The material was drawn from every walk of life and was written by numerous individuals, from uneducated herdsmen to highly skilled priests and kings. It consists of four sections.

The Pentateuch

The first section of the Old Testament consists of five books (Genesis—Deuteronomy). These writings contain the story of the beginning of the world up to the entrance of Israel into the promised land of Canaan. This collection of books is referred to as "the five books of Moses," "the Law," "the Pentateuch," or "the Torah." The Pentateuch was considered especially sacred by the Jews, since it contained the Ten Commandments and the history of the founding of their nation.

History

The second major section of the Old Testament contains basic historical material concerning the nation of Israel. It consists of twelve books, from Joshua to Esther. The narration goes sequentially through the capture of the land (Joshua); the history of the early nation (Judges, Ruth); the period of the united and divided monarchies (1 Kings—2 Chronicles); and the exile and return (Ezra—Esther).

Poetry

The third major section of the Old Testament contains books written mainly in poetic style. There is an epic poem (Job), a collection of hymns (Psalms), a collection of traditional wisdom (Proverbs), an ornate meditation on life and its vanity (Ecclesiastes), and a love poem (Song of Solomon). Hebrew poetry is different from English poetry in that it stresses a balance of ideas rather than sounds, rhythm, and images.

The Prophets

The fourth major section of the Old Testament contains the writings of the prophets of Israel. It is divided into two groups, the major prophets (Isaiah—Daniel) and the minor prophets (Hosea—Malachi). The words *major* and *minor* do not imply any value judgment but refer to the length of the books. Major prophets are long, and minor prophets are short. This section of the Old Testament contains prophecies concerning the coming of Jesus Christ.

THE PENTATEUCH

Genesis

Author: Moses
Date: c. 1400 B.C. or c. 1200 B.C.

Content

The Book of Genesis is a theological explanation of the beginnings of our universe. It tells about the lower orders of creation, like plants and animals; the human race; the nations of humankind; the selection of Abraham and one nation, Israel, to be the historical vehicle of God's redemption; the narrowing of God's purposes within that nation; and God's providential protection of one branch of that nation, the line of Joseph. There are other realities of our existence whose first appearance is noted in Genesis: evil, sin, rebellion, redemption, election, providence, and covenant. Other obvious realities that underlie the stories in Genesis, such as the creation of Satan or angels, are not described.

After a careful look at all this, it becomes clear that Genesis is a selective description of the origin of things. Moses, under the guidance of God, did not intend to discuss how *everything* came to be, but only things that contributed to a religious or theological understanding of history. This is not to say that Genesis is only "theological," whatever that may mean, or is untrue in any factual sense. When Genesis speaks factually it may be assumed to be true. But the facts primarily convey theological significance, rather than scientific or historical explanations. So, from a modern point of view, much is left out that would be of great interest to scientists, sociologists, psychologists, linguists, and others, but that would be of less value to theologians.

Theological Themes

Several underlying ideas in Genesis help us understand the diverse elements that otherwise might seem only distantly related. The first fundamental fact is that God exists. The world exists only because God *is* and because he chose to make it. The world does not *have to be*. If nothing else had ever been created, God would still *have been*, throughout all of eternity.

Second, everything depends on God and is his. Nothing can rightly claim to exist by its own power or purpose. God is in control and knows what he is doing.

Third, it is possible to reject God, but that is a very foolish and destructive thing to do. When God is effectively in control, all is well; when we choose to take charge ourselves, the result is evil, chaos, destruction, and pain. Sin is a tragic fact of human existence.

Fourth, in spite of our rejection of God, he has not rejected us. Even now, God is redeeming people on earth. Genesis shows that the essence of God is love and compassion for his lost creation.

Finally, God acts in history. His involvement does not begin when we die and go to heaven; it is happening now. In the midst of human history, with all its problems, struggles, and uncertainties, God's presence is certain. It was known by the patriarchs of our faith and, as Genesis teaches us, it can be known by us, too.

Outline

1. The initial creation *1:1–2:25*
2. The fall of humankind and its tragic results *3:1–5:32*
3. Crime and punishment: the flood and after *6:1–10:32*
4. The diffusion of people throughout the earth *11:1-32*
5. The story of Abraham *12:1–25:11*
6. The story of Isaac and Ishmael *25:12–27:46*
7. The story of Esau and Jacob *28:1–36:43*
8. The story of Joseph and the last days of Jacob *37:1–50:26*

Exodus

Author: Moses
Date: c. 1400 B.C. or c. 1200 B.C.

Content

The Book of Exodus continues the theme of redemption. We see redemption displayed in the nature of history itself and epitomized in Israel's particular history. The great drama shows God's people cruelly oppressed in a foreign territory, without benefit of a land or a human protector. God hears the cries of his people and sends a deliverer, Moses, to be the agent of his divine redemptive power.

The redemption pictured in the Book of Exodus is not just escape from oppression. God leads his people through a wilderness, providing for all of their needs. Then at Mt. Sinai he renews the covenant he had made with Abraham in Genesis, binding himself to all the people of Israel. Here laws are given, summarized in the Ten Commandments, which are a further evidence of God's love and concern for his people. Rules are given for all of life, and a religious structure (tabernacle, priesthood, regulations) is established.

The Book of Exodus therefore describes a "going on" as well as a "going out." After the Israelites went *out* of Egypt, they went *on* as a people in the wilderness, trusting the promises God gave at Sinai.

Theological Themes

The first significant theme in Exodus is the power of God. Nations, people, the sea, the natural elements, the wilderness—all are subject to his control. Second is the benevolence of God. He *cares* for his people, hears their cries, and rescues them. Third is the mystery of evil. It is present, both in Egypt and in Israel, but God's will is still being accomplished.

There is also a mystery in the relation between human and divine action. Pharaoh hardened his heart against God, but it is equally true to say that God hardened Pharaoh's heart.

Finally, there is the importance of our human existence as part of God's plan. He makes divine provision for all our needs in the form of guidelines (or laws). These laws relate to every aspect of our existence, showing us that God is concerned about all we do and are.

Outline

1. Bondage in Egypt and a deliverer sent *1:1–11:10*
2. The passover and exodus from Egypt *2:1–14:31*
3. Conflict and guidance in the wilderness *15:1–18:27*
4. The laws of God given and accepted *19:1–34:35*
5. The presence of God in tabernacle and priesthood *35:1–40:38*

Leviticus
Author: Moses
Date: c. 1400 B.C. or c. 1200 B.C.

Content
The Book of Leviticus served as a handbook for the ancient priests of Israel. Much of it is devoted to specific regulations concerning offerings, sacrifices, ritual purity, ordination, feasts, and festivals. There are also regulations that go beyond the religious institutions and that deal with the events of life. The implication of those regulations is that all of life is, in fact, religious. All that we do, whether in direct worship or not, is part of our relationship with God.

For example, we should not separate life into categories of sacred and secular, imagining that only the so-called sacred areas belong to God. God sees us as totalities, and all of life—work, worship, relationships, creativity, family—is important to him. That awareness is a source of great comfort in the book of Leviticus. It says that we should not worry that the writing is of no interest or value simply because these rules were formulated for a basically rural, agricultural, and ancient people, whereas we are, for the most part, urbanized, industrialized, and modern. Some may wonder about the rules themselves, which seem to have no bearing on contemporary life. A slight shifting of our mental gears should help us to overcome these problems. Looking at the basic idea rather than at the specific rule, we can see how each rule embodies a principle that is just as valid today as it was in Moses' day. In fact, it is amazing how current the ideas are. For example, the rule about sexual purity (15:1-33) may be seen as emphasizing the sanctity of sex and warning against its casual treatment. The need for such advice today is obvious.

Theological Themes

The theological themes that run throughout the Book of Leviticus are of great value for us to consider. The first important theological theme in Leviticus is that God is holy, and that he expects his people to be holy. This practical holiness is to govern our whole life.

Second, all of life should be viewed as God's. We must never imagine that we can cut God out of what we are doing. He is vitally concerned with all that we do.

Third, sin needs to be atoned for. The system of sacrifices established by God showed atonement in a graphic way and pointed to the great sacrifice eventually to be made in Christ. The blood of bulls and goats can never remove sin ultimately, the death of Jesus can and does do that.

Finally, our lives are to be lived horizontally as well as vertically. Our relationship to other human beings is just as important as our relationship to God. We are to love our neighbor as ourselves (19:18). Jesus said that this was of equal importance to loving God with all our hearts and, in fact, formed a commandment with it (Matt. 22:37-40; Mark 12:30-31; Luke 10:27).

Our devotion to God is part of a total understanding of life; all of life is God's. The Book of Leviticus was written to show the ancient Israelites, and us, too, how to live in a consecrated way before God.

Outline

1. Regulations about sacrifices and offerings *1:1–7:38*
2. The priesthood and the tabernacle *8:1–10:20*
3. Regulations about human life *11:1–15:33*
4. The great day of atonement *16:1-34*
5. Holiness before God as ethical living *17:1–22:33*
6. Festivals, feasts, and various other regulations *23:1–27:34*

Numbers

Author: Moses
Date: c. 1400 B.C. or c. 1200 B.C.

Content

The Book of Numbers narrates Israel's wide-ranging experiences in the wilderness. Jewish scholars from ancient times until today have referred to it by the title "In the Wilderness," which is the first word in the Hebrew text. Others refer to it as "Numbers" because the numbering of the people plays a prominent part in the book.

Numbers is a difficult book to outline because it consists of a collection of material that covers numerous events in Israel's wilderness life. There are problems, travels, judgments, rules, admonitions, complaints, battles, and conflicts. All of these are designed to show that human life is a series of difficulties that need to be dealt with by the grace of God. With such an approach, they can be turned into blessing.

The most significant events that stand out in the history of Israel in the wilderness are: the departure from Sinai; the sending of spies into Canaan, the Promised Land; the rebellion of the people in refusing to enter the land; the judgment of God, condemning the people to 40 years of wandering; the failure of Moses;

and the final victories of the people at the end of the 40 years.

Theological Themes

Certain things stand out theologically in the Book of Numbers. First is the fact that the tabernacle is central. It points to the centrality of God in the lives of the Israelite people. Tragically, Israel's worship later degenerated into outward formality—a lesson to all of us.

Second, God is in control of the whole situation. At no time is there any doubt as to who is running things. This is a comfort and a warning: a comfort, in that we can rest in God's power and sovereignty; a warning, in that rebellion is futile.

Third, it is clear that God demands obedience. We cannot simply ask God to do everything. He expects, and demands, that we fight battles, face enemies, and overcome obstacles—all with his help.

Fourth, life is seen as a pilgrimage. This theme is found in the New Testament's use of the Book of Numbers. Paul, in 1 Corinthians 10:10-11, says that all of these things were written for our admonition and learning.

Finally, it is clear that sin is a problem that needs to be faced among the people of God. It is sad to read that even Moses was not without fault before God, but the way he handled his problem is a lesson for us all. Earth is not heaven. That is certainly no news, but all too often we expect our lives to be without difficulty or temptation. Numbers shows us that such an expectation is wrong. We must always be on guard, lest we too "fall in the wilderness." The Book of Hebrews in the New Testament makes a big point of this, pointing to the "rest remaining" for the people of God and the struggles we must face here below (Heb. 4:1-16).

Outline

1. Organization of the people of Israel *1:1–8:26*
2. The memorial passover ceremony *9:1–10:10*
3. Wandering in the wilderness; various judgments and regulations *10:11–21:35*
4. Further wandering (in Transjordan); more judgments and regulations *22:1–36:13*

Deuteronomy
Author: Moses
Date: c. 1400 B.C. or c. 1200 B.C.

Content
Deuteronomy is the fifth book of the Pentateuch. It is something of a bridge between the earlier events of Israel's (and the whole world's) existence, and what follows after Israel's entrance into the promised land of Canaan. As such, it looks in two directions. It looks back to the events that brought Israel to the point of going in to the land to claim their inheritance, and it looks forward to what life will be like when they are there. It also shows us how Moses, the great leader of Israel, finished his years of leadership and then passed from the scene, handing over the reins to Joshua.

For the most part, Deuteronomy is a rehearsing of the laws and regulations given to the people while they were in the wilderness. Most of what is said can be found in the earlier books of the Pentateuch.

Theological Themes
Theologically, three things stand out in Deuteronomy. First, the importance of our remembering our past is emphasized. We need to look back to see where we have come from

in order to know where we are going. If we have made mistakes, we should not make them again; if we have done the right things, we need to keep on doing them.

Second, the importance of God's laws stands out. These rules were not given to be a burden to us, but to help us. God is an orderly Person and has planned things so that our lives run best when they are ordered too. It makes sense to obey God. He knows what is best for us and has shown us how to live.

Third, the importance of knowing God and worshiping him is stressed. There is only one God over all the heaven and the earth. He is to be worshiped. The wonder is that God not only allows this, but desires it. The highest act a person can perform is to find himself or herself in worship of God. Following directly upon our worship is service to those around us. Worship and service are two sides of the same coin according to Deuteronomy.

Outline

1. Review of Israel's wilderness wandering *1:1–4:43*
2. Review of Israel's laws *4:44–26:19*
3. Final acceptance of God and his covenant *27:1–30:20*
4. The last days of Moses *31:1–34:12*

HISTORY

Joshua

Author: probably Joshua
Date: c. 1350 B.C. or c. 1150 B.C.

Content

The Book of Joshua picks up where Deuteronomy leaves off. Moses is gone, and the role of leadership is Joshua's. Joshua had been one of the two spies (Caleb was the other) who had brought back a favorable report and urged the Israelites to enter the land. They would now enter after 40 years of wandering.

There are essentially three battle campaigns described in this book. The central campaign goes through Jericho and Ai and concludes with the treaty made at Gibeon. The occurrences in each of the three cities give us something to ponder: Jericho shows us the power of God; Ai shows us the wages of sin; and Gibeon shows us the foolishness of human beings. To leave the Canaanites in the land turned out to be a disaster a century or two later.

The southern campaign involves a coalition of kings led by Adoni-Zedek, king of Jerusalem. Joshua's army is able to defeat them by the direct help of the Lord.

The northern campaign brings Jabin, king of Hazor, into battle against Israel and sees his eventual defeat.

The land thus has rest from war (11:23) and the people of Israel now settle in to live in this new territory, which is apportioned to the twelve tribes.

Theological Themes

Numerous important theological ideas may be seen in the Book of Joshua. The focus on the centrality of God continues from the earlier books. God is God, and his will is being done. His power to act is also evident, as well as his control over the forces of nature and history. The holiness of God is evident in the judgment meted out to the Canaanites whose iniquity was now "full," but also in that Israel, too, was judged when it sinned. God is an absolutely impartial judge who will not regard one person above another. The mercy of God is also to be seen in the sparing of many from the horrors of war.

The importance of human involvement and response is a central theme of the Book of Joshua. God could have defeated his enemies directly had he chosen to do so, but he didn't. He used Joshua and the people of Israel. They made the decisions, marched through the land, fought the battles, set up the cities, and lived their lives. Through those actions God accomplished his will. It is important to keep both facts firmly together in our minds: God works; we work.

One other thing stands out: the necessity to make the right choices. The choice was thrust upon the new dwellers in the land: Choose whom you will serve, either God or the gods who were worshiped by the Canaanites. Joshua made the right choice for his people as an example for us. The temptation to follow false gods is just as strong today as it was back then.

Outline

1. The time of preparation *1:1–2:24*
2. The entrance into the land *3:1–5:15*
3. The conquest of Canaan *6:1–12:24*
4. The division of the land *13:1–21:45*
5. Settling under Joshua's leadership *22:1–24:33*

Judges

Author: unknown
Date: c. eleventh century B.C.

Content

After the conquest of Canaan, the Israelites divided up the land into sections and settled there tribe by tribe. They faced numerous problems: building houses, plowing the land, planting vineyards and trees, digging wells, and generally getting established as a nation. It was not easy, for the new settlers were attacked by invaders. To protect his people, God sent judges to lead them. These judges were not legal experts, but military leaders. They were especially empowered by God to gather an army, defeat the enemy, and rule over their district until things quieted down.

There are about fourteen episodes mentioned in the Book of Judges. One man, Abimelech, may not have been a judge, but his story is given anyway, probably to show what a disgrace he was. The book closes with two particularly grisly stories, one involving religious deceit and the other murder. They show what happens when people forget the Lord and rely on their own strength.

Theological Themes

The Book of Judges has a carefully followed pattern that is used to show how God works in history. Israel serves the Lord, then turns from God and falls away from his favor. To bring his people back, God allows them to suffer the consequences of their sin by punishing them through a foreign invader. Israel cries out to God, who sends them a judge or deliverer. Israel is then serving the Lord again.

A great deal can be learned from looking thoughtfully at this cycle of events. There is the fact of God's involvement in our lives as well as the fact of our own actions. When we do God's will, all is well; when we sin, we bring disaster on ourselves. Notice the mercy of God. No matter when the people cried out to him, he answered them. It is comforting to know that God is always there to hear our prayers.

Finally, notice the awful results of sin. When we choose to reject God's ways, terrible things result. The stories told are object lessons for us. It does not make sense to rebel against God. In the end, no one benefits from wrongdoing. This holds true even for God's people. After all, Samson was not a pagan, but an Israelite, and sin destroyed his life, too.

Outline

1. The conquest retold *1:1–3:6*
2. The stories of the judges *3:7–16:31*
3. The religious evil of the times *17:1–18:31*
4. The moral evil of the times *19:1–21:25*

Ruth

Author: unknown
Date: c. eleventh century B.C.

Content

The times of the Judges were extremely difficult years. That book concluded with the observation that anarchy reigned. No one was answerable to anyone else. The Book of Ruth shows a different side to this period, no doubt included to provide some relief to the otherwise almost completely bad situation.

It tells of a famine that drove Elimelech, his wife Naomi, and their family from Bethlehem to Moab to settle there. A young Moabite woman named Ruth married into the family and, after being widowed herself, refused to stay in her native land when her mother-in-law Naomi, also widowed by then, returned home. Her beautiful words, "Your people shall be my people, and your God shall be my God" (1:16), have inspired generations of struggling people. An act of kindness from a kinsman, Boaz, is recorded, providing an heir for the family of Elimelech. Boaz was to be an ancestor of David the king, and ultimately of Jesus himself. It is significant that Ruth, though born a pagan, was part of the ancestry of Christ.

Theological Themes

The religious truths found in this book relate more to practical life than to abstract theology. Loyalty, love, kindness, the value of persons, and the need to understand one another stand out. In the midst of the chaos then in the land, meaning could be found by returning to the first principles of simple truth. The Book of Ruth tells us that no matter how bad things may be, goodness can exist, if we are willing to make the effort.

Outline

1. In a foreign land *1:1-22*
2. Ruth and Boaz *2:1-23*
3. The redemption of Ruth *3:1–4:15*
4. The ancestors of David and Christ *4:16-22*

1 & 2 Samuel

Author: unknown
Date: probably tenth century B.C.

Content

These two books carry us into the period of time following the judges. Samuel, as the last of the judges, was the leader just before a king was appointed for the nation. Things were still chaotic, with new problems arising with regrettable regularity. The religious affairs of the nation were getting worse. The economic situation was bad. But most difficult of all was the presence of the Philistine army, which threatened to destroy the nation of Israel. In an epic battle, Israel was defeated and the Ark of the Covenant captured.

In the midst of this national confusion, Saul was appointed to be the first king. He was a strange figure, who alternated between doing the reasonable thing and insane acts of violence. Because of Saul's fear of others, David in particular, he spent excessive amounts of time fighting the wrong people. Rather than concentrating on ridding the nation of its enemies, he was in effect chasing out its friends. Things could not last long that way, and in the end Saul died an inglorious death in battle with the Philistines. It was a sad chapter in the history of Israel.

David was a different sort of king. He showed his military ability early, but he had remarkable administrative skills as well. When the time came, he was ready to structure the people along national lines and establish a government that would work. His biggest job was to defeat the Philistines in battle, and he did this. We are not told how, but it must have been a resounding victory because the Philistines never again presented any serious threat to Israel.

David was not perfect, however. At one point during a crucial battle he allowed his passions to overcome his reason and seduced the wife of one of his soldiers. He later deeply regretted that act, composing a psalm of repentance that even today is moving to read (Psalm 51).

Theological Themes

Several theological principles shine through the pages of these two books. Foremost is the continued fact that God is active in history to work out his purposes. He could impose his will on us, but he chooses not to do so. Rather, he weaves his purposes through our acts in such a way that our good is affirmed and our evil is judged. It is a great mystery how God can keep it all straight, but we are encouraged to believe that all will turn out well because God is in control.

Another important point is that God cannot be manipulated. When the Israelites were losing the war, they thought that bringing the ark into battle would bring them the victory. But God will not be forced like that. If our lives are not right, no amount of superficial piety will save the day.

God's love and forgiveness also stand out. On numerous occasions, God was forbearing toward those who offended him. The marvel of it all is that God does not deal with us according to our sins, but in mercy.

Outlines

1 Samuel

1. The life of Samuel *1:1–8:22*
2. The life of Saul until his split with David *9:1–20:42*
3. David in exile until the death of Saul *21:1–31:13*

2 Samuel

1. The rise of David as ruler *1:1–4:12*
2. The life of David as king of Israel and Judah *5:1–14:33*
3. Rebellion within the nation *15:1–20:26*
4. David's latter years *21:1–24:25*

1 & 2 Kings

Author: unknown
Date: sixth century B.C.

Content

After the death of David, his son Solomon ruled the still-united kingdom. His was a marvelous reign, and the nation prospered as never before or since. He built a magnificent temple for worshiping God, established a sound economy, expanded foreign trade, modernized the army, and built a series of fortifications for defense. Great as all this was, however, there were also problems. Solomon spent more than he took in, angered the various regions of his country, increased taxes to the breaking point, and took himself too seriously as a leader. So the good and the bad more or less balanced each other out, and as long as Solomon was around things went well. With his death, as is often the case with strong personalities, it all fell apart.

Solomon's son, Rehoboam, was not able to keep the kingdom together. Following some bad advice, he took a hard line with his critics and the nation split in two, along regional lines. The North became Israel, led by a man named Jeroboam, and the South was called Judah, led by Rehoboam.

Here we read of the various fortunes of the rulers of each kingdom down to the end of each. The northern kingdom was characterized by instability and bloodshed, but was visited by prophets from God, like Elijah and Elisha. Few of its rulers were very spiritual people, and the best remembered are its worst representatives, Jezebel and Ahab.

The southern kingdom had good and bad rulers, with periodic revivals taking place, notably under Hezekiah and Josiah. Prophets of great stature were sent to Judah, too, men like Isaiah and Micah.

Theological Themes

The theological principles found in these books are similar to those found in the books of Samuel. The control of God is emphasized. In the midst of the chaos of human history, God reigns supreme. God's rule is based on moral absolutes. When the Ten Commandments were given, they were not to be seen simply as good advice, but rather as rules to live by. Any person or nation that disregards them does so at their peril. To stand by idly when abuse of the poor, the innocent, or the helpless is taking place is to invite the judgment of God. The nations of Israel and Judah are testimony to this dread but solemn fact.

Another emphasis here is God's care for his people. Time after time, God sent prophets to plead with them to return to his ways. A refrain often heard was God's cry, "Why will you die, O Israel?" (Ezek. 18:31; 33:11). The tragedy was that it did not have to happen. Sin had come between God's people and God, but that did not cancel out God's love. To choose sin, however, was to choose death instead of life.

Another fact that stands out is the value of ordinary life. Throughout the centuries of Israel's and Judah's rise and fall, life went on with God at work in it. The people's biggest task, and ours, was just to live each day as it came, making the most of things, whether good or bad.

Outlines

1 Kings

1. The death of David *1:1–2:11*
2. The reign of Solomon *2:12–11:43*
3. The early history of the divided kingdom, to Jehosaphat and Ahaziah *12:1–22:53*

2 Kings

1. The divided kingdom to the fall of Israel *1:1–17:41*
2. The history of Judah until its fall *18:1–25:21*
3. Judah under Gedaliah *25:22-30*

1 & 2 Chronicles

Author: unknown
Date: fifth century B.C.

Content

The books of Chronicles seem boring to some people because of all the genealogies and because they cover the same material as Kings. Isn't that unnecessary? When properly understood, however, these Chronicles are important books. The key to understanding them is to remember that the Bible was written with a religious purpose in mind, not a political or historical one. This is not to say that history isn't there, or is false, but that whatever is said is recorded primarily for religious reasons.

The genealogies are important because the Messiah would someday be a human being. These records show the family histories of God's people as a whole, from which the Messiah came, as well as of his family in particular. They are also important because they show God's faithfulness through the passing centuries. His promises can be checked by looking at the records.

These books also lay heavy stress on Judah's history, rather than Israel's. This is because Judah represents the family of David and it was from David's line that the Messiah would come. The northern kingdom of Israel lived in a state of virtual anarchy, with assassinations and governmental turmoil almost a way of life. There was a measure of stability in Judah, with the rulers all coming from one family. Chronicles attributes this to religious faithfulness on the part of the South and apostasy on the part of the North. Not that God didn't love the people of Israel. He continually sent prophets to them to plead for their return. They would not come, however, and their destruction in 722 B.C. was the result of their hard-heartedness.

The religious aspects of Judah's history are also prominent. A lot of space is given to the temple, its worship, the priests, and the Levites. Stress is also laid on the revivals that took place under Hezekiah.

Theological Themes

Certain theological principles stand out in the Chronicles. First, there is the centrality of worship. So much time is devoted to the temple because it was to be central in the life of God's people. The same is true today. Where worship is routine or missing, whether in a nation or a person's life, spiritual death is just around the corner.

Second, the faithfulness of God is clearly seen. Throughout the many years when the nations' behavior merited only judgment, God remained true to his agreements (called covenants in Old Testament times) with his people. He remains true to them today.

Third, the justice of God is painfully clear. As much as he disliked doing it—and the Old Testament says this clearly—God had no other choice but to punish his people. This should be a warning to us all. God does not play favorites. All will be blessed and judged alike.

Finally, the need for daily watchfulness is evident. Too often our concern is for what *might* be, or for tomorrow. What we ought to do is watch out for today. Israel and Judah never seemed to learn that, and the result was their destruction. This need not happen to us, if we learn from their tragic examples.

Outlines

1 Chronicles

1. Genealogies from Adam to Saul *1:1–9:34*
2. The life of Saul *9:35–10:14*
3. The life and reign of David *11:1–21:30*
4. The organization of David's government *22:1–27:34*
5. The death of David and the inauguration of Solomon *28:1–29:30*

2 Chronicles

1. The life and reign of Solomon *1:1–9:31*
2. The history of Judah *10:1–36:21*
3. Footnote on Persia *36:22-23*

Ezra

Author: Ezra
Date: fifth century B.C.

Content

When the northern kingdom was destroyed in 722 B.C., its inhabitants were scattered throughout the ancient world and were lost track of. The land was filled by the Assyrians with foreigners, who became the Samaritans of Jesus' day. When the southern kingdom fell in 587 B.C., its prisoners were almost all taken and settled in one place by the Babylonians. As a result they did not lose their national consciousness. Although life in exile was hard for them, thoughts of Jerusalem sustained them over the many years that passed until they were allowed to return home by Cyrus, king of Persia. Psalm 137 is a beautiful but melancholy reflection on those days.

The book of Ezra picks up with the decree of Cyrus to let the people of Judah return home. Ezra was to be one of those who led a group of refugees back to establish the Jews in the land once more.

The first wave of settlers, who arrived in Palestine during the 530s B.C., did not find things easy going. Cities had to be rebuilt, farms plowed, walls constructed for protection, homes built, lives reestablished, and a new life begun. All of it was done in the face of opposition by enemy forces. The temple was also rebuilt and dedicated in 516 B.C. Ezra then led a new wave of refugees and was appalled to find the people so demoralized. A revival took place, and life was more tolerable for a while.

Theological Themes

The religious value of this book is to show us that although life is never easy, it can be lived with God's help. The struggles of God's people seemed overwhelming, but day by day they made it through. Their strength came from the Lord. If we could learn this lesson, we could make it through as well. No one ever knows what difficulties a day may bring, but reflection on Ezra and his times can bring renewed confidence. God has not changed, even if the way he accomplishes his purposes is different today.

Outline

1. The decree of Cyrus *1:1-11*
2. The census of the people *2:1-70*
3. The rebuilding of the temple *3:1–6:22*
4. Ezra's return *7:1–10:44*

Nehemiah

Author: Nehemiah
Date: fifth century B.C.

Content

This book is in some ways a parallel account to the one given by Ezra. Nehemiah was a trusted servant in the court of the Persian king but was committed to his nation and his own people. When he heard of the problems they faced, he requested permission to go to Palestine to help them. His specific concern was the rebuilding of the walls. Without walls, Jerusalem was helpless. Nehemiah must have been a man of immense energy and personal charisma because within 52 days the task was accomplished.

However, Nehemiah found more than just broken walls. He found broken lives. Discouragement had set in, God's commandments were being transgressed, and religious laxity, even among the priests, was common. The situation was not much better than it was before the nation had gone into exile. Realizing that something had to be done, Nehemiah took concrete steps to remedy the situation. The result was a reformation that brought the people, the aliens who lived in the land, and the priests back in line religiously and morally.

As a person, Nehemiah was a marked contrast to Ezra, who worked along with him.

Ezra was a rather quiet, scholarly type who wanted to reason things out. Nehemiah was a man of action who literally threw people out into the street if the occasion demanded it. Together they got the job done.

Theological Themes

Two things are significant in this book. First, there is the ever-present danger of backsliding. We must always be on the alert. If spiritual attrition could happen in Israel, it can happen in anybody.

Second, God uses people, and they don't all have to be alike. Ezra and Nehemiah were different personality types, but God used them both. He will use us, too, if we let him.

Outline

1. Jerusalem's walls rebuilt *1:1–7:53*
2. The people's repentance *8:1–10:39*
3. The nation reformed *11:1–13:31*

Esther

Author: unknown
Date: fifth century B.C.

Content

The Book of Esther tells a straightforward story. It takes place in Persia, where Jews were to be found after the return to Palestine had taken place. Not everyone went home. For over a thousand years the largest concentration of Jews outside Palestine was to be found in the region where they had formerly been exiled.

The king of Persia married a Jewess named Esther, who uncovered a plot against her people led by Haman, the prime minister. Genocidal actions were common in antiquity and have carried down to our own day, as was the case in Nazi Germany. When Esther and her cousin Mordecai brought the plot to the attention of King Ahasuerus, Haman was deposed and replaced by Mordecai. Those who had taken part in the aborted plan were all executed, and the Jews narrowly escaped a frightful slaughter. To commemorate the event, a feast called Purim was established.

Theological Themes

Some persons have objected to the presence of this book in the Bible because it does not seem to have any specifically theological themes, nor is the name of God mentioned in it. Religious content, however, is there; it is below the surface, rather than obviously presented. The main point is that ordinary life is not ordinary but filled with eternal significance. Events fit into a normal pattern of cause and effect, but woven through it all are the hidden purposes of God. Human choices are of great importance and have profound consequences, whether for good or evil. The Book of Esther says in effect: Watch what goes on and do not be deceived by appearances. More is happening than you think.

Outline

1. Esther becomes queen *1:1–2:23*
2. The plot of Haman *3:1-15*
3. Haman's plot uncovered *4:1–7:10*
4. The consequences of Esther's bravery *8:1–10:3*

POETRY

Job

Author: unknown
Date: perhaps as early as tenth century B.C.

Content

Job, one of the most complex and interesting books in the Old Testament, deals with a profound human theme. Why do people suffer, if God is in control? That problem has exercised the best minds of virtually every society from the beginnings of civilization until today. The book itself, a very long and highly structured poem, is about a man named Job who lost all that he had within a short period of time. He found himself an outcast, waiting for death near the city dump, when some of his former friends came to comfort him. The hidden backdrop to the story is the will of God and the sneering challenge of the Devil.

The first set of speeches made by Job's friends has the general theme that Job is sinful. The all-wise, all-powerful God, they say, is only giving him what he deserves. All three friends speak—Eliphaz, who is a kindly mystic; Bildad, a rather unsympathetic traditionalist; and Zophar, a narrow dogmatist. These three men represent different approaches to the problem of suffering, as does Job himself. Job replies to them all, ending with a touching appeal to God ("Though he slay me, yet will I hope in him" 13:15), and longs wistfully for an afterlife of peace and tranquility.

The second set of speeches hammers on the theme that divine judgment is coming for the wicked. It never seems to occur to these three speakers that there might be a *mystery* to human life and that simple answers might not work. Job agonizingly replies, reaching a high point (some would even say the watershed of the book) in 19:23-29, where he affirms his deep personal faith in God and the future. "In my flesh I will see God."

The third set of speeches extols God's wisdom and control of life, implying that Job is an ignorant fool who has no right to reply to God. Job reaffirms his position that he does not deserve what is happening to him.

A new person enters the scene, Elihu, who approaches the subject from a different angle. In essence he says that pride has entered Job's heart and a mysterious correlation exists between that and the suffering that Job is having to endure.

Before anyone can speak, God replies to them all. Job's friends, Elihu, and even Job are all wrong. None of them has all the facts, and consequently none of them is in a position to make a final judgment. Attempts to justify God fall short for lack of knowledge; attempts to justify oneself fall short for lack of honesty.

Only God is in a position to put everything together correctly, and Job is invited to learn this lesson. When we have nothing left but God, only then do we realize that God is enough.

After Job learned that lesson, his fortunes were restored and he was comforted and consoled. "The Lord blessed the latter part of Job's life more than the first" (42:12).

Theological Themes

Many theological points are made in this book, but two stand out: the majesty of God and human finitude and need. If we could simply keep these two realities in their rightful place, we would need little else when crises arise in life. The solution to our problems comes when we see God for who he is.

Outline

1. Prologue: scene in heaven *1:1–2:13*
2. First set of speeches *3:1–14:22*
3. Second set of speeches *15:1–21:34*
4. Third set of speeches *22:1–31:40*
5. The speech of Elihu *32:1–37:24*
6. The reply of God *38:1–42:6*
7. Epilogue *42:7-17*

Psalms

Author: principally David, but also others
Date: tenth century B.C. and later

Content

Psalms is probably the best-known and best-loved book of the Bible. It has provided more personal comfort, imagery, hymns, and poems than any other book that has ever been printed.

The Psalms were written over a long period of time, perhaps 600 years. A large number of them were written and collected by King David (hence the name "Psalms of David"), but many were added to the collection after his day. The book was used much as it is used today. The Israelites used it in their public worship. They read from it or sang from it, depending on the circumstances. Some of the psalms were written for special services, such as the coronation of the king. Thus, many of the psalms were hymns, anthems, and special music, sung by the congregation, choir, or both. The Psalms were used privately for personal devotion. Almost every possible emotion or situation is covered in them.

Theological Themes

The Psalms contain some of the richest theology in the whole Bible. Underlying the psalmist's outlook is the concept of the power of God. God is in control of this universe. Although it may appear at times that things have gotten out of hand, this is not so. God is beyond our knowing, but we are not beyond his power. He acts at the right moment, in the right way. Our job is to learn how to trust him.

God's providence, or effective working, is also prominent in the book. He works like a master craftsman, weaving his will in and out of our free choices, so that in the end we have a blend of divine and human activity. Indeed, he works *in* our free choices as well, accomplishing his own good purposes. This should give the believer great comfort and courage; beyond all disappointments and problems we can know that God is there, caring, and able to work out his loving purposes.

The tenderness of God is constantly emphasized. Like a father who pities his children, or a hen who gathers her chicks under her wings, so God deals with us. He remembers how he made us, he knows that we are but dust. Consequently he does not expect what we cannot give. He is compassionate and merciful, fully aware of every possible angle to every situation. He knows how to make allowances for human frailty.

God is also depicted as just. No wrongs will go unrighted. No evil done to God's people is unseen. In due time, all will be made right. The temptation either to give up on the one hand or to join the evildoers on the other must be resisted with the strength that God provides. Evil will not win because the justice of God will not let it.

The proper response of God's people is also evident. We are to live lives of prayer, praise, humility, thanksgiving, and faith. Each one of these ideas, explored in depth in the Psalms, should be the fabric of our existence. In them we find the secret of living.

The beauty of the world, the value of life, the goodness of the natural order, and the sheer joy of living are also described. From the grass that grows beneath our feet to the loftiest thoughts in our heads or the highest stars in the sky, the majesty that God wrote into the world is undeniable. It is there for all to see. However, there is also mystery. Ambiguities exist that are unresolvable apart from God. Glory, mystery, ambiguity—these are the essence of human life, and God is their source and answer.

Outline

1. Book 1 *1–41*
2. Book 2 *42–72*
3. Book 3 *73–89*
4. Book 4 *90–106*
5. Book 5 *107–150*

Proverbs

Author: principally Solomon, but also others
Date: tenth century B.C. and later

Content

The Book of Proverbs embodies the collective wisdom of Israel. Usually attributed to Solomon, it is a collection of sayings that reflects Israel's views about how one was to live life in the presence of God. To live this way was wise; those who taught these epigrams were "sages" or wisemen.

The idea of wisdom is common in the Old Testament. In its fullest and highest sense, wisdom belongs to God alone. He is the originator of all life. He knows everything that occurs or could occur. To him belong the earth, humanity, all other living things, the stars, heavens, and angelic hosts. All are evidence of the wisdom of God. In one place it is even said that wisdom was a mastercraftsman along with God (8:22-31). God's wisdom guides the affairs of nature and of humankind, and his ways are past knowing. His ways are not our ways. Consequently we should never second-guess God in order to attempt an explanation of things.

God has revealed some of his wisdom to us. When speaking of wisdom in this way, the Bible uses the term in three ways. Sometimes a skill is described as wisdom. A person who has the technical ability to do something like build a ship or a building is called wise. Sometimes the art of making the right decisions is called wisdom, whether moral or nonmoral. Preachers need wisdom to succeed, but so do architects; both are called wise when they make right choices. Finally, wisdom among human beings is the art of right living. It includes all aspects of our lives and begins with "fear" (respect) of the Lord. It is a religious and practical knowledge that unifies our lives in the presence of God.

The Book of Proverbs sums up this idea of wisdom with a collection of aphorisms that cover every aspect of life—relation to parents, growing up, serving God, resisting temptation, practical advice, seeking the truth, the folly of riches, situations to avoid, the knowledge of God, the perfect wife, to name just a few.

Theological Themes

The central theological idea of Proverbs is that God is creator and ruler. He made the world to function a certain way, and if we have any sense at all we will look to him as supreme. Life is filled with mysteries, but God understands them all and invites us to turn to him for guidance. A second theme, related to the first, is that all of life can be redeemed. Since God made all of life, all of it may be offered to God. Not a single phase of legitimate human existence is outside God's concern. A third theme is that serving God makes sense and leads to a full and satisfying life. This stands to reason. If God made life to function best by living a certain way, to live that way produces meaning and fullness in our lives. Finally, only fools choose death. Two roads are open before us: the way of life and the way of death. The wise person chooses life; the fool chooses death. The way we go depends eventually on us.

Outline

1. Introduction *1:1-7*
2. Thirteen lessons on wisdom *1:8–9:18*
3. Book 1 of Solomon's wisdom *10:1–22:16*
4. Collections of the sages *22:17–24:34*
5. Book 2 of Solomon's wisdom *25:1–29:27*
6. The wisdom of Agur *30:1-33*
7. The wisdom of Lemuel; the perfect wife *31:1-31*

Ecclesiastes

Author: probably Solomon
Date: tenth century B.C.

Content

The author of Ecclesiastes calls himself Koheleth (the preacher). His exact identity is not known, but traditionally he is identified with Solomon, king of Israel. Ecclesiastes is a difficult book to understand, partly because it is structurally disjointed, but mainly because it seems to have two different sets of ideas in it. It reads a bit like a collection of sermon notes rather randomly put together, leaving it to the reader to decide what to make of it all.

Basically there are two interpretations to the book. One sees the book as a pessimistic statement of life that represents the true view of the preacher. He has tried everything, and all is vanity. His conclusion is to live life to the fullest, die, and pass into a state of eternal nonexistence where there is no feeling or consciousness and from which there is no return. Interpreters who adopt this view explain the optimistic passages, those that imply a belief in God or in justice, as later additions. Such an interpretation has a certain appeal to it, especially in our skeptical age, but it runs so counter to everything else the Old Testament says that it ought not to be taken too seriously.

The other interpretation sees the book as a sermon, or a series of sermons on the vanity of life. The preacher adopts a secularized point of view in order to show that if one lives according to those rules, all he or she can expect is disappointment. In this view, the statements that speak of the meaninglessness of life represent the secularism of the preacher's day, and not his own view. His outlook is expressed in the passages that speak of belief in God and trust in him. In order to make his point, the preacher shows that life lived apart from God, no matter how desirable it might seem, is in the end frustrating and unsatisfying. He shows that wisdom, material possessions, sensual pleasure, wild parties, power, and prestige cannot satisfy. The best a secular philosophy can come up with is something like this: Life is short, full of uncertainty, meaningless, and void of any real peace of soul. Because death ends everything, we should simply live now and when we die be done with it. Having said all this, the preacher has proved his point; life lived apart from God is a hopeless affair.

But that is not the whole story. Throughout the book, running alongside the secular philosophy of despair, is the assertion that God sees through our pretensions and sorrows and will meet us in love if we want him (3:17; 8:12; 11:9; 12:14). Koheleth's conclusion to the whole matter is this: "Fear God and keep his commandments" (12:13). That is not a bad evangelistic message.

Theological Themes

Two theological points stand out in the Book of Ecclesiastes. First, the power and redemption of God are the ever-present background for all that is said. God is there, always available, waiting for the moment when wayward seekers after pleasure realize that this world cannot really satisfy. Second, there is the fact that life is not able to meet our needs if we go at it in the wrong way. Not being ultimate, it cannot provide for our ultimate longings and needs. If, however, we see life as under God's control, it may be used by us in the proper way. The world makes a very good servant, but a very hard taskmaster.

Outline

1. Preface *1:1-11*
2. The futility and oppression of life *1:12–4:12*
3. The vanity of life in all its forms *4:13–7:14*
4. Secular philosophy and its failure *7:15–10:3*
5. Summary of the vain life and how to overcome it *10:4–12:14*

Song of Solomon

Author: probably Solomon
Date: tenth century B.C.

Content

This book represents one of those grand surprises that pop up from time to time in the Bible. Because most people understand the Bible to be a book about religion and spirituality, it cannot be imagined that a book dealing with a theme like human love could be found there. The Song of Solomon tells about a Shulammite woman and her beloved. There is the mutual admiration expressed by each one for the other, as well as descriptions of their physical love. It is a beautiful and touching picture, going to the heart of human emotion and life.

Over the centuries, there have been numerous interpretations of this book. Some commentators have seen in it a vivid picture of the love of God for Israel or the love of Christ for the church. By looking at it in this way, these writers reinterpret the sensual imagery on a more spiritual plane. This book, however, gives no evidence that it is discussing the subject of God's love. Other interpretations say that it deals with ancient ritual, dramatic presentations, or liturgical rites. Those views also seem a bit overdone.

Probably the best way to take the Song of Solomon is at face value. It deals with human love and the beauty of it. When God made humankind he made us "male and female" (Gen. 1:27). That is a simple and fundamental fact of existence. That two people should love each other, and that their love should express itself physically ought to embarrass no one. The Song of Solomon celebrates that love in what could be called a collection of love poems or reflections.

Theological Themes

The basic truth taught in this book is that the structures of our humanity (psychological, physical, emotional, etc.) were created and blessed by God. The proper human response is to accept ourselves as we are in glad thankfulness for the way God made us.

Outline

1. The dream of the bride for her beloved *1:1–3:5*
2. The arrival of the bridegroom *3:6-11*
3. In praise of the bride *4:1–5:1*
4. Night thoughts of the bride *5:2–6:3*
5. The beauty of the bride *6:4–7:9*
6. The beauty of love *7:10–8:14*

THE PROPHETS

Isaiah

Author: Isaiah
Date: eighth century B.C.

Content

The Book of Isaiah is one of the best-known books of the Old Testament. It is the book most frequently quoted in the New Testament and the one used most frequently by Jesus. Throughout the history of the church it has been used in worship, in hymns, and by theologians. The reason for its popularity is twofold. First, it contains the clearest Old Testament presentation of the gospel. The depiction of sin, the helplessness of the sinner, the marvelous love of God, his provision of a Savior, and the call to repentance and faith are all to be found there. Second, the book abounds with memorable phrases and images which have become part of our general church vocabulary or hymnody.

Isaiah wrote during a period of impending doom in Judah, in his time the southern half of what had been the nation of Israel. The mighty Assyrian army was devastating the northern regions and Isaiah's nation appeared to be next. Isaiah urged Hezekiah the king, against all logic, to cast himself on the Lord for protection, promising that God would be true to his word by sparing Judah. When Hezekiah dared to trust God, a plague broke out in the Assyrian camp, killing most of the army and forcing the Assyrians to withdraw. Thus the tiny nation of believers was spared. Isaiah's book covers those difficult times with messages, sermons, historical accounts, exhortations, and prophecies.

Theological Themes

The theological content of the Book of Isaiah is one of the high points of the Old Testament. Paramount in the book is Isaiah's stress on the holiness of God: God is called "The Holy One of Israel." God's holiness is the foundation of all his dealings with the world. Because of this, Judah could rest secure; God would never do anything that was not just and fair. Isaiah tried to draw Judah's attention to the covenant (binding agreement) that God had made with his people. They were his. He might find it necessary to judge them for their sins, but he would never abandon them. If they got carried away into captivity, a remnant would return to pick up where their ancestors left off. In wrath, God would remember his mercy.

Perhaps the most prominent theme in Isaiah's message has to do with the coming Messiah, God's Servant. Four extended psalms, or poems, deal with the Suffering Servant of God. In them the ministry of Jesus is foretold; at another level they are descriptive of Judah, too, which as a nation was also

God's servant: 42:1-7; 49:1-7; 50:4-11; 52:13–53:12. The Servant is to suffer for the world, establish justice, provide salvation for the nations, be a light to the Gentiles, teach the truth to all who will listen, give sight to the blind, offer release to the prisoners, be a covenant to the world, treat the weak with compassion and care, dispense God's Spirit, bear the sins of the world, make intercession for sinners, provide the knowledge of God to those who seek it, and secure peace for all people. All of these dimensions have been fulfilled by Jesus Christ.

Finally, the Book of Isaiah offers a promise of salvation in some of the most beautiful imagery in all of the world's literature. The message concerns God's forgiveness and mercy, freely offered to all who respond in faith.

Outline

1. Judgment pronounced on Judah *1:1–5:30*
2. The call of Isaiah as a prophet *6:1-13*
3. Judgment and blessing pronounced on Judah *7:1–12:6*
4. Judgment pronounced mainly on other nations *13:1–23:18*
5. The apocalypse of Isaiah *24:1–27:13*
6. Judgment and blessing on Judah, Israel, and Assyria *28:1–39:8*
7. Future blessing and comfort for Judah *40:1–66:24*

Jeremiah

Author: Jeremiah
Date: sixth century B.C.

Content

The prophet Jeremiah is one of the best-known figures in the Old Testament because of the biographical detail to be found in his book. In most other instances the man is subordinated to the message so that little is known about the preachers as individuals. In Jeremiah's case, his life was so woven into what he said that it is hard to separate the two.

Jeremiah lived during the darkest days of Judah's history, spanning the reigns of five kings, and ending with the destruction of Jerusalem in 587 B.C. He called for a national renewal of faith during the days of Josiah (640-609 B.C.) and was partly successful. When Josiah was killed in battle, he was succeeded by a king who submitted to international blackmail. Jeremiah continued his stern message of repentance, urging the people to accept the heavy hand of God as punishment for their sins. For this he spent many of his remaining years in jail. When the nation finally fell to the Babylonians, Jeremiah was spared and allowed to live in the rubble that was Jerusalem, where he continued to preach. Ultimately carried off to Egypt as a hostage, he died in exile.

Theological Themes

Jeremiah the prophet is a triumph of faith and courage. In the midst of terrible difficulty, he spoke with conviction and strength. He was virtually the only one who saw clearly what was going on. His dedication to the call of God was such that he never wavered. Because of this, he is a monument for all times of how to live when darkness surrounds us.

The foundation of Jeremiah's message was his conception of God as sole creator and ruler of all that is. God acts according to his own will, he knows human hearts, he helps those who trust him, he loves his own. He demands that his people respond with obedience and faith. Because God knows what he is doing, the desperate situation in which Judah found itself was not outside God's knowledge or plan. If the people of Judah would only accept God as Lord, God would show himself as their deliverer in due course.

A second point stressed by Jeremiah was human responsibility to God. The people had no one to blame but themselves. They were trying to put the blame on their parents, the surrounding nations, the prophets who pointed out their faults, or even on God—but never on themselves. Jeremiah wanted them to see that restoration can come only when we are able to accept the fact that we are accountable for our own lives. Granted that all those things might be factors that influence us, they can never be used as excuses for our wrongdoings.

Jeremiah also urged Judah to trust in God alone. For too long the people had been trusting in their military abilities, their money, or even their own religiosity. They thought that mere attendance at religious services was enough to make them pleasing to God. It was a rude shock to be told that God was not impressed with how much money they had or whether they "went to church" or not. God would allow no rivals, Jeremiah said.

Finally, Jeremiah opposed the false religion and preachers of his own day. Truth must exist within our hearts. Someday God would make a new covenant with his people (31:31), which would write the law inside their lives, not on tablets of stone. Jesus came to introduce that new covenant and establish true religion forever.

Outline

1. The call of Jeremiah *1:1-19*
2. The sins of Judah outlined *2:1–13:27*
3. Jeremiah's ministry to Judah *14:1–33:26*
4. Jeremiah and the last days of Judah *34:1–19:18*
5. Jeremiah after the fall of Jerusalem *40:1–41:18*
6. Jeremiah in exile in Egypt *42:1–52:34*

Lamentations

Author: Jeremiah
Date: sixth century B.C.

Content

Although the Book of Lamentations is anonymous, there has never been any real doubt that Jeremiah was its author. It was written by an eyewitness of the destruction of Jerusalem, lamenting that fact—hence its name, Lamentations. It is a funeral song, written in the rhythm and style of ancient Jewish dirges. The first line of the two-line couplets has three parts to it and the second line only two. The repetition of this rhythm, with the third element systematically missing, is a stylistic reminder of the absence of the loved one, in this case, the city of Jerusalem.

To the Jews of the Old Testament, Jerusalem's fall was the loss of everything—their temple, priesthood, sacrificial system, capital city, nation, and large numbers of their loved ones. For the survivors of the destruction, it meant a forced march of about 2,000 miles to Babylon, where they then had to live in exile, servitude, and misery.

Theological Themes

The spirit of the Book of Lamentations goes beyond merely weeping over the past. Here we have an implicit warning that to transgress is to invite disaster. The prophets had predicted that God would judge the sins of his people if they did not repent. Now, the ashes of the city were testimony to the fact that God had spoken and was true to his word. History was thus a vindication of God and his righteousness. It was also a declaration of the wrath of God, never a popular concept. Most people choose to emphasize the softer side of God, and properly so, but that understanding must never obscure the fact that God is not to be trifled with. When we ignore the needs of those around us, trampling on justice, God will step in to right those wrongs. It is a grim reminder that it does not pay to rebel against God.

Lamentations has another side, however. Although the nation of Judah is cast down, it is not without hope. The people may yet trust God and find pardon. God is one whose mercies are renewed every morning, whose faithfulness is great (3:19-39). We see the value of patience, prayer, and confession of sin. God does not hold grudges and is willing to start over anytime we are willing to acknowledge our errors and resubmit ourselves to him.

Outline

1. Judah's desolation and sorrow *1:1-22*
2. The vindication of God *2:1-22*
3. Judah's hope in God's mercy *3:1-66*
4. Judah's future glory *4:1-22*
5. A final prayer *5:1-22*

Ezekiel

Author: Ezekiel
Date: sixth century B.C.

Content

Ezekiel was born near the end of Judah's existence, perhaps as early as 620 B.C. He was from a priestly family, but was called by God to be a prophet. He was deported to Babylon in 597 and was settled in the village of Tel-Abib on the river Chebar. Five years later, he received a formal call to become a prophet to the exiles and the remaining Jews in Jerusalem, although he never actually went there. Ezekiel's message was at first rejected, but later, when a messenger from Jerusalem arrived, announcing that the city had fallen, the people began to listen. Ezekiel's prophecies had come true (33:21). He now gave himself to preaching about the coming restoration, just as earlier he had given himself to preaching about the coming judgment.

Ezekiel was an extraordinary person in at least three respects. First, he had remarkable powers of imagination, seen in his descriptions of the heavenly beings and the coming age. Second, he was possessed of supernatural gifts that allowed him to see events in Jerusalem in detail, even though he was over 1,000 miles away. Third, he was a man of great courage and determination. He was not discouraged by the rejection of his message, but kept preaching the truth. When he was finally vindicated, he did not gloat but kept to the task God had given him.

Ezekiel saw himself as a shepherd, watchman, and defender of God. As a shepherd, his task was to look out for his people, tending them from within. He saw himself as a symbol of the Great Shepherd who was to come, the Messiah, Jesus Christ. As a watchman, he was to warn of the coming judgment. Just as a military guard peers into the dark of night to see the approaching enemy, so Ezekiel peered into the darkness of time and cried out that judgment was coming. As a defender of God, he explained that the nation fell, not because God was weak, but because the people were sinful.

Theological Themes

At the heart of Ezekiel's message is the transcendence of God. The prophet's opening vision, with all of its strange imagery and figures, emphasizes this. God is so far above his creation that words cannot fully describe him. As a result, strange figures of speech are needed to convey the message that God is exalted above creation. Ezekiel exhausted his powers of description trying to explain who God is. Ezekiel also emphasized the Spirit of God. The other prophets had used the phrase "the word of the Lord" to emphasize the presence and activity of the Lord. Ezekiel said that the Spirit of God was leading him. The purpose of the Spirit's leading Ezekiel was to give the people a message that would lead them to God. Their problem was that they had lost touch with God; they no longer knew God personally. To know God in this sense is to acknowledge God as sovereign over history and over ourselves. God must be acknowledged as *our* God.

Ezekiel also brought a message of judgment. Because Judah had sinned against God, God's judgment must come. Judah had disobeyed God's laws, profaned his temple, desecrated his Sabbath, listened to false prophets, indulged in uncleanness and defilement, and entered into foreign alliances.

Finally, Ezekiel had a message of restoration. The nation would rise from the ashes of its death like a dead body from the grave. That hope is vividly portrayed in the vision of the dry bones (ch. 37). A new era is coming, in which God will reign supreme.

Outline

1. Prophecies of doom for Judah and Jerusalem *1:1–24:27*
2. Messages to the pagan nations *25:1–32:32*
3. The renewal of life and the ideal age *33:1–39:29*
4. The new temple and the new age *40:1–48:35*

Daniel

Author: Daniel
Date: sixth century B.C.

Content

Daniel's name means "God is my judge." He was either of royal descent or from a distinguished family of Jerusalem. He was taken into captivity by Nebuchadnezzar during the reign of Jehoiakim, which would make it before the fall of Jerusalem in 587 B.C. Because his potential was recognized, he was allowed to study in Babylon along with other Babylonian youths. His course of study consisted of language and science, probably in preparation for royal service. During that time of training he was allowed by his adviser to live on vegetables and water, rather than eating rich food and wine. Daniel's dedication made him a better student than his Babylonian counterparts.

In the second year of his reign, Nebuchadnezzar had a dream that only Daniel was able to interpret. As a result, Daniel was given a position of authority over the Babylonian scientists (magicians). After Nebuchadnezzar's death (562 B.C.), Daniel apparently lost his job because of the change of government. During Belshazzar's reign, however, Daniel was restored to government as Third

Chief Governor after interpreting some mysterious handwriting on the wall during a banquet. Daniel held that post during the subsequent reigns of Darius and Cyrus the Persian. Daniel was obviously an intelligent, righteous person, trusted even by pagans in high places. He was protected by God in miraculous ways and was in a position to write a book such as this. About his later years and death we know nothing.

The Book of Daniel consists primarily of a series of prophetic dreams and visions. Some historical material is also there, but as background for the prophetic material. Daniel interpreted Nebuchadnezzar's first dream (2:1-49) to mean that four great kingdoms would fall. Nebuchadnezzar's second vision (4:1-37) pointed out his vanity and pride.

Daniel's dream (7:1-28) in many ways parallels Nebuchadnezzar's first dream, only fantastic beasts represent the kingdoms of the world, rather than different metals in a gigantic statue. In this dream a figure called the "son of man" appears (v. 13). (In the New Testament, Jesus used this term with reference to himself.)

Daniel had another vision (9:24-27), perhaps the most important in the book. It speaks of a time when God's work would be completed. Many Christians see this prophecy as fulfilled in Christ, the one who atoned for iniquity and will bring in everlasting righteousness. Daniel had other visions (8:1-27; 11:2-20; 11:21–12:3), also prophetic, dealing with the events of world history.

Theological Themes

We can see four elements in the message of Daniel. First, God is all-knowing. He can predict future events, and he revealed some of those secrets to the prophets. Second, God rules over human affairs. This does not mean that we are not free to act, but it does mean that God works in and through our choices. This gives us confidence to live because ultimately no one can defy God and get away with it. God is still on the throne. Third, evil will ultimately be overcome. Although God's enemies may get the upper hand at times in history, the final chapter has not yet been written. When it is, God will come out the victor, along with those who have chosen to live for him. Finally, God's Messiah, Jesus, is vital in his plan for the world; Daniel had an intimation of that redemptive mystery.

Outline

1. Life in Babylon *1:1-21*
2. Early visions in Babylon *2:1–6:28*
3. Daniel's visions of world empires *7:1–8:27*
4. Daniel's visions about history and salvation *9:1–12:13*

Hosea

Author: Hosea
Date: eighth century B.C.

Content

Hosea was a prophet to the northern kingdom of Israel for about 50 years. His ministry began during the reign of Jeroboam II, making him a contemporary of Amos, who also preached to the North, and of Isaiah and Micah, who preached to the southern kingdom of Judah. Hosea lived to see the fall of his nation to the Assyrians in 722 B.C.

Hosea's unhappy family life became a tragic model for his prophetic message. He married a woman (Gomer) with the highest ideals of marriage. Hosea 1:2 says "a wife of harlotry," but this is in retrospect, considering what she had become by that time, not what she was at marriage. If she had been impure at marriage the analogy to Israel would not have fit—Israel was pure and became impure, as Gomer had done. His first child, a son, was symbolically named Jezreel, pointing to the coming judgment. The second child, a daughter named Lo-Ruhamah ("she-who-never-knew-a-father's-love"), was not Hosea's, and the father would never be known. The third child, a son named Lo-ammi ("not-my-kin") was not Hosea's child either. When Hosea reflected on the pain of his marital situation, he was reminded of the pain his faithless nation had inflicted on God. Just as Hosea loved Gomer in spite of her infidelity, so God loved Israel.

After six years Gomer left home to become a prostitute. Even then Hosea did not cease caring for her. After a time she slipped to the point of actually being sold into slavery. Rather than let that happen, Hosea bought her himself, bringing her back home.

The book consists of two unequal sections. The first, chapters 1–3, is mostly biographical, detailing the events of Hosea's turbulent life. The thought is difficult to follow because the narration is a mixture of Hosea addressing his wife, God addressing his nation, and combinations of both. The second section, chapters 4–14, consists of addresses, reflections, prophecies, sermon notes, comments, and pronouncements of doom. Because they are undated, it is difficult to know whether they came before or after the fall of Samaria in 722 B.C. Probably some are before and some are after.

Theological Themes

The message of Hosea stresses the steadfast love of God, who continues to care for his people despite every provocation imaginable. There was simply no reason why God should continue to love his people, but because his love was steadfast he did. A touching illustration of this can be found in 11:1-4. A second theme is that God takes the lead in his dealings with his people. Grace is mercy extended to those who do not deserve it. Like Gomer, Israel qualified on that count. Third, Hosea emphasized the reality and enormity of Israel's sin. He was not blind to the fact that what Gomer and Israel were doing was wrong, and he could not ignore this in the name of sentimentality mistaken for love. True love sees what is really at stake and calls things by their right name. What Israel and Gomer were doing was sin and would ultimately be their undoing. Fourth, Israel's basic problem lay in having "rejected knowledge" (4:6). Knowledge in this instance means understanding, not so much recollection of facts. Israel did not understand God at all. Neither did Gomer understand Hosea. Fifth, repentance must precede renewal. God asked Israel to acknowledge its sin and return to him.

Outline

1. Hosea's life as prophecy *1:1–3:5*
2. Hosea's message of judgment to Israel *4:1–13:16*
3. Promise of blessing if Israel repents *14:1-9*

Joel

Author: Joel
Date: probably eighth century B.C.

Content

Little is known about the prophet Joel except that his father's name was Pethuel, he probably lived in Jerusalem, and he prophesied to the southern kingdom of Judah. His book has been considered the earliest prophetic book written, the latest prophetic book written, or just about anywhere in between. Joel made an effort to round out his rhythm and to balance his sentences. His book is one of the most elegant literary pieces in the Old Testament.

An atmosphere of impending doom pervades this prophecy. The major nations of the world, Babylon and Assyria, are not mentioned, so we are left to guess whom Joel had in mind as he thought about the coming judgment. A plague of locusts had just swept through the land, providing a background for Joel's visions of doom. As the book opens, we hear the sound of a mighty army of insects stripping the vegetation bare.

Theological Themes

Using the plagues of locusts as an example, Joel meditates on the coming wrath of God. His words concern the present existence of

Judah, but then shade off into discussing a future judgment, usually associated with the end of the age. This twofold approach provides the student of the Bible with an excellent example of what is known as prophetic "foreshadowing." Two future events, although separated by many years, are spoken of as though they were one event: the events are telescoped together, giving the appearance of being one. Joel called the plague of locusts "the Day of the Lord" (1:15–2:1, 2, 31). A second theme in Joel is that, after judgment, a time of blessed prosperity may be expected (3:17-18). Like the other prophets of Israel and Judah, Joel emphasized that God stands ready to forgive, if people repent. God is gracious and slow to anger, abounding in steadfast love. If Joel's contemporaries would genuinely change their lives and attitudes ("Rend your heart and not your garments") God would withhold judgment from them (2:13). Finally, Joel foresaw a future outpouring of the Holy Spirit (2:28-31). The apostle Peter later quoted these verses from Joel's prophecy as foretelling the day of Pentecost (Acts 2:16-21).

Outline

1. The plague of locusts and the judgment of God *1:1–2:27*
2. The day of the Lord: blessing and judgment *2:28–4:21*

Amos

Author: Amos
Date: eighth century B.C.

Content

Amos prophesied just 30 years before Israel fell to the Assyrians (722 B.C.). The 50 years preceding Amos were a time of relative calm and prosperity for both Israel and Judah. In the midst of that apparent prosperity, however, an inner sickness was developing. The poor were being oppressed, the weak were intimidated, justice was ignored. Religion was a pretense, corruption a way of life.

Amos was not technically a prophet. Rather, God called him to leave his occupation as a shepherd and tree farmer in order to make God's will known to Israel. The fact that he was from a small town in the South and was not formally educated made his mission to the North difficult. He courageously pointed out that God was not impressed with outward pietistic show, devoid of moral content. Amos stuck to his calling in the midst of adversity.

Theological Themes

Amos depicted God as the ruler of history—past, present, and future—as righteous, patient, and long-suffering, impartial. God seeks fellowship with his people and demands a righteous life on their part. Amos points out the grace that God had shown to Israel. He selected Israel for special blessing; he gave them the Law; he established a place of worship in the temple and gave them the sacrificial system; he fought their battles; he worked miracles; he led them through the wilderness; he prepared a place for them in Canaan; he sent them prophets and special leaders; he gave them wealth, food, clothes, and homes; he caused business and commerce to flourish. And he gave them his Word.

Amos catalogued the sins of Israel: cruelty, genocide, dishonesty, anger, greed, lawlessness, sexual excess, desecration of the dead, rejection of the prophets, violence, robbery, selfishness, injustice, deceit, and pride.

Amos drew attention to the judgment to come. He pointed out that God weeps over people's sins, takes no delight in judgment, and offers repentance if they want it. But he is clearly not optimistic about the prospects of Israel's actually repenting.

Finally, Amos tells the people of Israel what God requires. They are not to bring more sacrifices or offerings to the temple, but they are to seek justice, good, honesty, and the well-being of all their people.

Outline

1. Judgment on the nations *1:1–2:16*
2. Three prophetic sermons *3:1–6:14*
3. The visions of Amos *7:1–8:8*
4. Epilogue *8:9–9:15*

Obadiah

Author: Obadiah
Date: sixth century B.C.

Content

The shortest book in the Old Testament, Obadiah deals with the relationship between Judah and its southern neighbor, Edom. Obadiah is prophesying the fall of Edom because of its inhumane treatment of Judah. The fact that the two peoples were distantly related is important in understanding the book. Esau, to whom the Edomites traced their ancestry, was the brother of Jacob, to whom the Judahites traced their ancestry. Esau rightfully was to inherit the blessing of his father, Isaac, but sold it for a bowl of porridge. Jacob, though deceptive, received the blessing instead. Because of Esau's act, he became a symbol in Judah of a profane person, insensitive to spiritual values.

Judah's descendants settled just north of where Esau's descendants settled, and relations between the two groups were never very cordial. There were frequent border clashes between the two countries, usually with Judah winning. The two major cities of Edom were Sela and Bozrah. Teman, mentioned by Obadiah, was in the southern part of Edom. Sometimes the whole country is called Mt.

Esau, in contrast to Mt. Zion, which stood for Jerusalem or Judah.

When the Babylonians arrived, Edom saw its chance. The Edomites followed the Babylonians in, letting them do most of the fighting and then took whatever they wanted for themselves. That behavior earned them the scorn of the prophet and the punishing hand of God. Edom was destined to fall, said Obadiah, and fall it did, in 312 B.C. So two nations fell for their sins. Judah, however, would learn its lesson and be allowed to return to start over. Edom would remain a heap of ruins forever.

Theological Themes

The message of Obadiah is simple. Edom will be destroyed for its indifference, cowardice, and pride, as will all who choose to live in defiance of God.

Outline

1. Prophecy against Edom *1:1-14*
2. The day of the Lord and Judah's blessing *1:15-21*

Jonah

Author: Jonah
Date: eighth century B.C.

Content

The prophet Jonah is known primarily for his extraordinary encounter with the "big fish." Born in a small town in Israel during the reign of Jeroboam II (782-753 B.C.), Jonah's mission was to preach repentance to one of Israel's dreaded enemies, Assyria, in its capital city, Nineveh.

When God commanded Jonah to leave his native city in Israel to go to Nineveh and preach, Jonah was furious. Why should God care about those pagans? So Jonah deliberately took a ship headed in the opposite direction. A great storm arose and Jonah accepted responsibility for the danger, requesting that he be thrown overboard. A great fish swallowed him and after three days he was disgorged onto the land. Chastened, Jonah then went to Nineveh to preach. When the people of Nineveh repented, Jonah was resentful. He sulked outside the city. God then taught him a lesson, using a plant. The point was, if Jonah could have pity on a bit of vegetation, couldn't God have pity on an entire city full of people?

Most of the discussion that surrounds the Book of Jonah concerns whether or not these events could actually have happened. Some argue that it reads like an extended parable, and hence was not meant to be taken literally. Others believe that it is better to let the account speak for itself. The book looks like history, with the prophet being named and the events of his life being rather carefully described. That it took a miracle for Jonah to survive his long stay inside the fish is not denied. If God could create a world, fish, and Jonah, he certainly could handle a matter like that (1:17). Other arguments used against the book, such as the size of the city or the unlikelihood of the city repenting, are more apparent than real. All in all, it is best to take the book as a startling but true account of God's offer of repentance to the Assyrian nation at Nineveh.

Theological Themes

The purpose of the Book of Jonah is plainly stated: "Should I not be concerned about Nineveh, that great city?" (4:11). The compassion of God for all people, even Israel's enemies, is at the heart of the book.

Outline

1. Jonah's refusal to follow God's command *1:1-17*
2. Jonah's repentance *2:1–3:10*
3. Jonah's remorse at the city's acceptance of God *4:1-10*
4. The pity of God for Nineveh *4:11*

Micah

Author: Micah
Date: eighth century B.C.

Content

Micah was born about 25 miles southwest of Jerusalem in Judah. His ministry saw the arrival of the Assyrian army, the fall of Damascus in Syria, the war between Israel and Judah, the conquering of Galilee, the destruction of Samaria and the northern kingdom of Israel, and Sargon's defeat of Egypt. It was a violent, unsettled period of time.

The Book of Micah is a collection of sermons and prophecies, largely arranged by topic. The style varies; sometimes Micah is harsh and vigorous, at other times tender and compassionate. His language is straightforward and forceful.

Micah's message was directed primarily to Judah. He was particularly concerned to defend the oppressed. He saw a society in which wealthy landowners took advantage of the poor, oppressing them unmercifully. Farmers, peasants, and small landowners were harassed. He saw the city as a symbol of national corruption: corrupt law courts, government officials, religious leaders.

The basis for Micah's message was the righteousness of God. Micah stressed that God demands righteous actions from us, not outward show. He summed up what God requires of us—to do justice, love kindness, and walk humbly before God (6:8).

Theological Themes

Micah presented a message of judgment. God will bring judgment on the land to destroy it if it does not mend its ways (3:12). Micah also gave one of the most detailed Old Testament accounts of the coming Messiah (5:2-15). The redeemer will come from Bethlehem and be a human being (not an angel). He will have been pre-existent from eternity, will bring together a righteous group of believers, will introduce a kingdom of righteousness on earth, and will care for those in need. The New Testament sees this as fulfilled in Jesus Christ.

Micah proclaimed a universal reign of peace that will be for all people. Swords will be beaten into plowshares and spears into pruning hooks. It will be a time of peace, prosperity, and plenty (4:1-5). God will rule over all, and war will cease to exist.

Outline

1. The wrath to come *1:1-16*
2. Judgment on evildoers *2:1–3:12*
3. Future blessedness *4:1-5*
4. Prophecies of blessing and judgment *4:6–5:1*
5. The Messiah to come *5:2-15*
6. God confronts the nation *6:1–7:20*

Nahum

Author: Nahum
Date: seventh century B.C.

Content

Nahum, born in Elkosh, in Judah, was a prophet whose primary ministry was to the city of Nineveh. Jonah had been sent by God about 100 years earlier to preach repentance to the Ninevites, and a large portion of them had responded favorably. The intervening years, however, brought a change of heart as well as a change of government, and Nineveh went back to its old ways. God therefore gave Nahum the task of preaching judgment to the Assyrian capital sometime between 664 B.C. and the city's fall in 612 B.C. Although his message was directed to Nineveh, there is no evidence that Nahum ever went there in person.

Theological Themes

Nahum's message is one of coming judgment for the Ninevites. Their sins will be punished: specifically their idolatry (1:14), arrogance (1:11), murder, lies, treachery, superstition, and social sins (3:1-19). For all of this the city will be destroyed. Nineveh was, he said, a city filled with blood (3:1), a graphic description of the awful depths to which the nation of Assyria had sunk.

The foundation of Nahum's message is that God rules over all the earth, even over those who do not acknowledge him as God. Nineveh's gods and goddesses were nothing according to Nahum. The only God who exists holds us all accountable, whether we know it or not, whether we accept it or not. God alone is God. The Ninevites would soon see that to trust in idols is to trust in wood and stone.

Nonetheless, Nahum pointed out, God was willing to save the city if they repented. God is always seeking the lost, is slow to anger (1:3), is good (1:7), and is a stronghold to those who trust in him (1:7). God sends good news to those who will listen (1:15), a theme later taken up by the New Testament writers when describing the work of Jesus and the preaching of the *gospel* (a word that means good news).

Outline

1. A prophecy of judgment *1:1-15*
2. The fall of Nineveh *2:1-13*
3. The reason for Nineveh's fall *3:1-19*

Habakkuk

Author: Habakkuk
Date: seventh century B.C.

Content

Habakkuk prophesied during the last days of Judah, just before its destruction by the Babylonians in 587 B.C. In the year 605, at the great battle of Carchemish, the Babylonians defeated what was left of the old Assyrian army and the Egyptians. That opened the way for Babylon as the new world power to exert its influence along the major trade route that ran from the Fertile Crescent down to Egypt, running right through Judah. It was only a matter of time before Judah would feel the heavy hand of Babylon, and Habakkuk, with prophetic insight, knew that.

Habakkuk did not cry out against the sins of Judah as such, but came at the problem in a different way. Because he was convinced that God is good and all-powerful, he wondered out loud why God allowed these things to happen. Granted Judah was sinful, but God was strong enough to do something about it, so why didn't he? That kind of approach to the problem is almost unheard of in the Old Testament. The Book of Job looks at evil in somewhat this fashion, but Habakkuk is alone among the prophets in doing so.

Theological Themes

Habakkuk got his point across by using the question-and-answer method; he asked a question and God supplied the answer. Question #1 is found in 1:2-4. It asks, in essence, why God allows evil. Justice has failed, the poor are oppressed, violence is to be seen on every hand, and God seems to let it happen. Answer #1 is in 1:5-11. God responds that he is about to enter in and punish the sin he sees in Judah. He will accomplish this by using the Chaldeans (Babylonians) as the rod of his anger. They are terrible in warfare, proud, worshipers of their own strength, merciless to captives, and destined to win.

That raised an even more serious question in Habakkuk's mind. How could God use an even more evil nation to punish Judah (1:12–2:1)? God is so pure that he cannot look on evil, yet he is about to make use of the Babylonians. How could that be? God gave a two-part answer. In 2:6-19 the practical, historical aspect of the question is answered. Babylon, too, will be judged. In 2:2-4 the theological aspect of Habakkuk's question is answered in some of the most important words to be found in the Bible—the just shall live by faith. God told Habakkuk that human logic might fail, but God's wisdom will not. Even though we cannot understand the way things are going, that doesn't mean there is no answer. God has the answer and the one who would be just (righteous) before God must learn to trust him and live by faith. In one sense this is not so much an answer to the question as an invitation to realize who God is. That made Habakkuk understand he had been talking too much. The proper attitude to have in the presence of God is silence: the silence of quiet acceptance, not the sullen silence of resignation to our fate (2:20). Next comes one of the most beautiful prayers in the Old Testament, ending with Habakkuk's affirmation of faith (3:17-19). We can rejoice in the Lord even if everything is taken away from us. Because that actually happened in Habakkuk's case, he is an example of how to face the worst that life has to offer us.

Habakkuk shows how God was able to use the Babylonians, even though they did not acknowledge him as God. God is Lord of all the earth, even over those who refuse to accept him as such. It doesn't really matter to God, because he is the only God who exists.

Outline

1. Introduction *1:1*
2. The problem of Judah's sin *1:2-4*
3. The judgment of Judah's sin *1:5-11*
4. Habakkuk's second question *1:12–2:1*
5. God's answer and call to faith *2:2-19*
6. Habakkuk's triumph of faith *2:20–3:19*

Zephaniah

Author: Zephaniah
Date: shortly before 621 B.C.

Content

Zephaniah was the first of a series of prophets sent by God to the southern kingdom of Judah before its fall in 587 B.C. and after the fall of the northern kingdom of Israel in 722 B.C. Isaiah and Micah had lived to see the fall of Samaria, the capital of the northern kingdom, but had died before Zephaniah's time. Zephaniah was followed by Jeremiah, Habakkuk, and Ezekiel, all of whom had a special message to Judah in the South. Regrettably, that nation, too, paid no attention to the warnings sent from God.

The historical situation went something like this. After the death of Hezekiah, a righteous king in Judah, his son Manasseh ascended the throne. He was a thoroughly evil man who rejected his father's ways and allowed wholesale corruption back into the land. He was also instrumental in reintroducing pagan religious practices like Baal worship, astrology, spirit worship, and child sacrifice. Manasseh persecuted the prophets and suppressed the true worship of God. Jewish legend has it that he was party to executing the prophet Isaiah, although this cannot be proven one way or another. His son

Ammon was just as bad, but his grandson Josiah (639-609 B.C.) tried to reverse the trend toward disaster. In 621 Josiah made sweeping reforms, partly because of Zephaniah's warnings.

Theological Themes

Zephaniah concentrated on denouncing the evil that abounded in the land, with the dire warning that if Judah did not repent, all would be lost. He also brought further insight to the concept of the "day of the Lord." Popular opinion assumed that the day of the Lord meant vindication for them in the face of their enemies. Zephaniah told them it meant judgment first for them and then for their foes. The prophet ended with a promise of restoration (3:9-20), looking beyond a mere return to the land to a time of universal blessing for the whole earth.

Outline

1. General prophecy of God's judgment *1:1–2:3*
2. Judgment on specific nations *2:4–3:8*
3. Future blessings promised *3:9-20*

Haggai

Author: Haggai
Date: 520 B.C.

Content

After the fall of Jerusalem in 587 B.C., the survivors were carried off into captivity in Babylon. An international upheaval, resulting in a change of world leadership, then put Cyrus the Persian in charge of what was left of Babylon (539 B.C.). One of the first things Cyrus did was to allow former captives to return home if they wanted to go. A sizable number of Jews returned, although by no means all of them, and work was begun in the restored community. It was a difficult time. There were walls to be built, houses to construct, a temple to dedicate, farms and fields to plant, forests to clear, roads to build, and an army to raise for protection. What to do first? After a zealous start on the temple in Jerusalem, interest waned and work ceased in 536 B.C. After sixteen years of inactivity and divided interests, the prophet Haggai preached his message, demanding that work be resumed on the temple so that God would have a fit dwelling place. His book consists of four messages, all preached in 520 B.C. The first was directed to Joshua, the religious leader, and Zerubbabel, the civil leader. It denounced the people for spending time on their own amusement while the temple lay in ruins. The second encouraged those who wanted to build, but were afraid the results would be insignificant. The third and fourth messages denounced the present state of corruption and promised God's protection, if the people responded to God.

Theological Themes

The basic message of the Book of Haggai is simple: our spiritual state is more important than our material state. We must make a home for God, whether on a hill (then) or in our hearts (now), if we expect God to bless us.

Outline

1. Message to Joshua and Zerubbabel *1:1-15*
2. Word of encouragement *2:1-9*
3. Things will change for the better *2:10-19*
4. God will preserve the leaders *2:20-23*

Zechariah

Author: Zechariah
Date: between 520 B.C. & 500 B.C.

Content

Zechariah preached to the restored community at the same time that Haggai did. The people had returned home from exile only to find an enormous task confronting them. There were homes to build, walls to erect, fields to plow, forests to clear, roads to build, and a temple to construct, all in the face of strong opposition from the people who had moved into the land after the Jews had been carried away into captivity. Haggai encouraged the people to rebuild the temple, while Zechariah preached on more general issues. The heart of the book is the eight visions:

Vision 1. Riders on colored horses through a grove of trees. This is interpreted as pronouncing judgment on the nations, with God being the rider of the main horse. Israel would be comforted in three ways: The temple was to be built, the city of Jerusalem was to be rebuilt, and the outlying districts were to overflow with prosperity.

Vision 2. Four horns that scattered Jerusalem. The four horns were four kingdoms (Assyria, Babylon, Egypt, and Medo-Persia), all of which would fall in recompense for having destroyed Jerusalem.

Vision 3. A young man with a tape measure to measure Jerusalem. This was an encouraging vision about safety in Jerusalem. The young man is forced to stop measuring the city for the rebuilding of its walls, because God would be a wall of fire around it to guard it from the surrounding nations.

Vision 4. Joshua the High Priest in rags before the Lord. This graphic vision depicts the grace of God. Joshua is not fit to stand before God wearing the rags of his self-worth. Satan accused him, only to be silenced by God who provides clothes fit for the divine presence. Only God can make us presentable in the courts of heaven, by an act of grace and mercy.

Vision 5. Two trees feeding oil into a central bowl supplying seven lamps. This vision shows the never-failing supply of strength from God (the trees), the agent of supply (the Holy Spirit), the human agents used by God (Joshua and Zerubbabel), and the fact that the job gets done. The key verse in this vision is 4:6. "Not by might nor by power, but by my Spirit, says the Lord Almighty."

Vision 6. A flying scroll. This is a public declaration that the sins of Israel will be punished. It shows that even in the restored community sin was still a problem and needed to be dealt with.

Vision 7. A flying bushel basket. The basket, when opened, reveals the sins of the nation. They are removed when two stork-winged women carry the basket away.

This shows both the presence of sin in the community and the fact that God can forgive it.

Vision 8. Four chariots between two copper mountains. This obscure vision speaks of the certainty of God's will being done. The mountains represent the strength of God's decrees, and the chariots represent the divine agencies through which God accomplishes his purposes.

The collection of miscellaneous visions is important because they refer to the Messiah as the Good Shepherd, rejected by his people, sold for 30 pieces of silver, riding into Jerusalem in triumph on a donkey, and mourned for as an only son. The New Testament sees all this as having been fulfilled by Jesus.

Theological Themes

The basic message of Zechariah concerns the accomplishment of God's will. God is in absolute control of life and history. By symbol, vision, image, and statement, Zechariah hammered home the point that we need never fear if we are doing God's will. The Messiah (Jesus Christ) will come to represent God and will do God's will. First he comes in weakness, but later as a sovereign Judge.

Outline

1. Introduction *1:1-6*
2. A series of eight visions *1:7–6:15*
3. Miscellaneous oracles *7:1–14:21*

Malachi

Author: Malachi
Date: between 450 B.C. & 425 B.C.

Content

This book, like the prophecies of Haggai and Zechariah, was addressed to the restored community of Israel, but came considerably later. Another wave of refugees had come, and Ezra and Nehemiah were also on the scene.

All was not well in the nation of Israel. Pagan and other questionable practices were common in the land. There was religious unconcern, greed, corruption in governmental circles, and marriages to foreign women (which meant introducing foreign gods back into the land). The priesthood especially was a problem. Religious matters had become routine, lacking any real significance, either for the priests or for the people of the land. The lack of concern here was called nothing less than robbery of God.

The book consists of two sections. The first deals with the sins of Israel and the second with promised blessings and judgments. It is set up as a series of questions and answers, much like a courtroom scene, with Israel asking rhetorical (and often self-justifying) questions and God answering. The questions are as follows: How have you loved us (1:2)? How have we despised your name (1:6)? How have we defiled you (1:7)? Why do we profane the covenant of our fathers by breaking faith with one another (2:10)? How have we wearied him (God) (2:17)?

Theological Themes

Malachi singled out the priests for judgment. They knew what God required. The sacrifices were unworthy, there was no sincerity in their service, their duties were performed in a lazy manner, and they had no real commitment to God. If the religious leaders go wrong, why should the people be any different? Second, Malachi said, the people had not learned the lesson of the exile. They had gone into captivity because of their sins and had returned bent on following their old ways. Judgment would come again if the nation continued to reject God. Third, a message of hope was proclaimed for the future. The judgment day of the Lord was coming, but on it the Lord would purify the priests and the temple, would redeem the righteous, and would usher in the reign of God. All this would be preceded by a messenger who would prepare the way of the Lord. The New Testament understands this messenger to be John the Baptist.

Outline

1. The sins of Israel itemized *1:1–2:17*
2. Promised blessings and judgments *3:1–4:6*

More Books for Christian Living

BIBLE INDEX POCKETBOOK. This easy-to-read index contains references to more than 1000 important subjects. Useful with any translation.

THE BIBLE TELLS ME SO: God's Promises for Kids. The Bible's answers to questions kids ask most.

PARENT'S PROMISE POCKETBOOK. Hundreds of verses highlight the blessings and challenges of parenting.

PERSONAL PROMISE POCKETBOOK. Discover how God's promises and purposes correspond to many of your needs. The Four-Step System will help you claim and retain these verses.

POCKET GUIDE TO THE NEW TESTAMENT. Handy outlines and summaries of content and theological themes for each book of the New Testament.

PROMISES FOR GRANDPARENTS. Strong comfort from Scripture for those who are growing older and want to build a godly heritage.

STUDENT PROMISE POCKETBOOK. Special answers from God's Word for students and young adults, featuring the Four-Step System that helps you personalize and claim God's promises.

Order from your favorite bookstore or write:

Harold Shaw Publishers, Box 567, Wheaton, IL 60189